EXPLICIT
M O V E M E N T

2 1 D A Y

I N T E R A C T I V E

J O U R N A L

EXPLICIT MOVEMENT
21 DAY INTERACTIVE JOURNAL
By Michele Okimura

Copyright © 2018 by Explicit Movement
Published by Explicit Movement
Printed in the United States of America

ISBN: 978-0-692-12786-5

Cover Design & Internal Layout: Ahava Design
Photos by Unsplash.

explicitmovement.org

IMAGINE A PLACE...

BY MICHELE OKIMURA

Imagine a place.
A place where heaven's light exposes darkness
So that nothing is hidden.
A place where God's Beloved are invited
To dance and embrace the Light.

Imagine a safe place.
A place where vulnerability is welcomed,
Safeguarded, and honored.
Where voices are heard
And genuine love transforms lives.

Imagine a resting place.
Homes. Where children and youth
Freely entrust their hearts to their parents.
A safe home, where answers to difficult issues
Are discovered together… with no shame.

Imagine an honoring place.
Where sexual integrity is embraced.
Where purity is guarded and valued.
A place where battles to protect the marriage bed are won.
Where God's design for sexuality is celebrated and sacred.

Imagine a healing place.
A place where no person feels alone, unwanted, unloved.
A place where each understands their immense value.
Where lives and broken relationships are restored.
Where God's forgiveness, grace, and power abound.

Imagine a heavenly place.
Where individuals, families,
Cities and nations experience true transformation.
Because the Father made Himself known.
Because Heaven kissed earth through His people.

Imagine a place.
Where no one hides in the darkness,
Or in the loneliness of their personal closets.
But is welcomed and beckoned forth
To partner with God and help change the world.

WELCOME TO THE 21 DAY JOURNEY

Welcome to Explicit Movement's interactive journal! It is our hope and prayer that you will encounter God daily in profound ways.

In serving you, our team's desire was to create a space and a place each day for you to experience Him...a safe place, a resting place, a healing place, a heavenly place, and a place where you feel honored.

This is a different journal of sorts that includes short devotional messages from the Explicit Movement Team and dear friends of Explicit Movement. There is power in their stories, just as there is power in your story. As you become acquainted with the 19 authors you will soon meet, we pray that God's Presence will embrace you and transform you. Each author has courageously chosen to be vulnerable and real with you, trusting you with a precious part of them.

On this journey, you will also meet five special bible characters who will introduce you to each new section. Each will mentor you through deep personal moments in their lives.

You have heard the sentiment, "A picture speaks a thousand words." The journey through these pages will also be a visual experience. Photographs will display God's hope, joy, peace, and love to you. Each word written, and each photo chosen has been covered in prayer in hopes that God would use such creative elements to impart His daily message to you.

Following each devotional, a 'challenge' is provided to help springboard you to connect with the Lord and to apply what you just read to your life. Space is also provided for you to write or sketch your reflections.

At the end of this journal, we also provided small group discussion questions for each devotional should you decide to go through the journal with others.

May you find joy in the journey!

Blessings,

Michele Okimura
Explicit Movement, Director

CONTENTS

Longings deep within us emerge to seek
a path of fulfillment like the waters of a
bubbling spring find a pathway to flow.
But where does the path take us? In this
section, explore the deeper undercurrents
of your soul that can lead you to the
only One who will meet your ultimate,
innermost need.

———

/desire_

You wanna know a secret? Well, most of my business is already out there on the streets, so I guess I don't have too many secrets. Growing up, I didn't think my life would look like this. I never wanted to be a woman with five husbands. When the first one left, and then the next, and the next…I didn't know what to do. I didn't even know if the guy I was with at the time was going to abandon me too. Every girl prays she will get a husband that adores her, respects her, protects her, but that was not how the cards fell for me. I was far from being adored and I certainly wasn't respected. Protected? Well, let's not get into that.

Desire. My heart was full of desire for love. For validation. For life. For hope.

I met this man Jesus, and everything changed. He asked me for a drink of water that day and actually talked to me—the one person in town that people hated. It's like he saw me, the one who felt invisible. He knew everything about me that was shameful, yet his eyes held no judgement. Only compassion. That one conversation we had changed my life. How He did that, I don't know. I just know the shame, the pain, this dark thing I felt following me everywhere just disappeared! I felt alive for the first time.

Come now! Meet this man Jesus who knew everything about me and knows everything about you! This man Jesus who says to you, "YOU are My Great Desire!"

✖

A creative narrative written by Tinasha LaRaye based on
The Samaritan Woman in John 4:1-28

Day 01

THIRST

Writing by Mark Palompo

I was in the final stretch of Ka'au Crater Hike. Exhausted, my shoes were cement as I dragged them one step after another and my mouth tasted like glue. So thirsty. Back at my car, water ran down my chin and shirt as I gulped greedily from the jug I had left behind. I relished the moment of cool, refreshing water quenching my thirst. "Ahhh..."

When was the last time you were thirsty?

I've often found that my deepest thirsts come from my soul and not my physical body. Like the girl who posts half-naked selfies at the gym, I've thirsted for 'likes' and attention. Or how the guy who keeps texting a girl after numerous rejections might be thirsty for affection and acceptance, I too thirst for acceptance, approval, and newness.

In years past, I would try to satisfy these thirsts through pornography and relationships. I sat at my screen for hours, drinking in the images before me. I spun from one broken heart to the next. Never satisfied, my spirit had become a parched land in drought.

One night, everything changed. Far from home, I sat in an unfamiliar house surrounded by drunken strangers. These were her friends but to me they seemed foreign. Even hostile. We had been dating for a year, but I knew she didn't feel the same way I did about commitment. Being here was another desperate attempt to win her affection. As the night went on, guys began asking her to hook up with them. Filled with jealousy, I pulled her aside and asked her to leave with me. She told me, "You can leave. I just got here." The feelings of betrayal and rejection knocked the wind out of me. I slipped out and walked aimlessly down a lonely street. I was so tired of empty pursuits. Years of wandering, and I had nothing to show for it. In desperation, I cried out to God for help in that darkest hour. Jesus met me at my well.

HOPE

It was as if Jesus reminded me that His offer still stood. That even after all my years of running, I had not been disqualified from the Spirit of His Living Water. I surrendered my life to Him and immediately it was like a wellspring of hope and promise erupted within me.

Will you meet Jesus? He is waiting for you. His Living Water will satisfy your deepest thirst and wash away any rejection or shame. It's a process and journey, but He desires to transform your life, filling you until you overflow!

"Jesus answered, "If you drink from Jacob's well, you'll be thirsty again and again, but if anyone drinks the living water I give them, they will never thirst again and will be forever satisfied! For when you drink the water I give you it becomes a gushing fountain of the Holy Spirit, springing up and flooding you with endless life!" John 4:13-14 TPT

Challenge
Reflect on these questions:

> What are the longings of your heart?
> How do you meet those desires?
> What do you do to comfort yourself?

In the blanks below, list the longings of your heart that come to mind. What do you desire and hope for?

_____

_____

_____

Take a moment and imagine Jesus coming right to you, offering a cup of His refreshing, life giving water He prepared just for you. Jesus comes to you at this moment and hopes with anticipation that you will receive His gift. He offers you hope, truth, wisdom, compassion, understanding, and direction!

Open your hands in front of you right now and allow the Lord to fill you as you rest awhile in that position. Journal your reflections.

Plan a time where you can be alone with God for 15 minutes. In a private setting, listen to the song, "O Come to the Altar" by Elevation Worship. As you meditate on the words being sung, envision Jesus standing before you. Make each word of the song your prayer of offering to the Lord. When you are done, you can record any feelings, thoughts, or words you experienced.

_____

_____

_____

IN SEARCH

Writing by Richard De La Mora

It doesn't make sense; this wasn't supposed to happen to me. How could a young man who grew up privileged, in the suburbs of Santa Barbara, California, want nothing more than to commit suicide? I was driven by the fear of when I might have my next panic attack. I tried everything to make them go away. I thought maybe if I could achieve fame or make a lot of money, then I would finally be happy, and if I was happy, then the panic attacks would leave me alone. I was in search. In desperate search for peace to calm the turbulent ocean within my soul. The enemy offered me a taste of fame and fortune. I had become a successful disc jockey. I was on high demand. It looked like I had it all on the outside, I was spinning records at the most prestigious places, but on the inside, I was spinning out of control. My search for fame and money left me more lost and confused than before.

Then on 6-6-06 while having a severe panic attack, I cried out to God in desperation, "If you are real, then show me! If not, I don't want to live anymore!" Five minutes later, my uncle, Pastor Sergio, called me and said he was driving up to Santa Barbara from San Diego. One hour later, we met up, and he led me to accept Jesus as my Lord and Savior. My life was forever changed. I finally found the peace I was longing for.

Here's what the enemy does—he robs us of our identity, so we don't fulfill our destiny. He wants us to focus on everything but Christ, because he knows that only God, our Creator, can replenish our dehydrated souls.

God knows you. He shaped you, formed you, and beautifully designed you with great purpose. Everything you have been searching for can be found in Christ. We will remain empty and in search until we realize everything is found in Him.

I encourage you to seek God. Time spent in God's Presence is never wasted. Search for His loving touch in your life each day. He will begin to speak to you, fill the void in your heart, and refresh you with His Living Water that truly satisfies.

"Don't be pulled in different directions or worried about a thing. Be saturated in prayer throughout each day, offering your faith-filled requests before God with overflowing gratitude. Tell him every detail of your life, then God's wonderful peace that transcends human understanding will make the answers known to you through Jesus Christ." Philippians 4:6-7 TPT

Challenge

Our hearts are all in search for peace, joy, purpose, and meaning. You and I are not alone in having the tendency to fill our lives with activities that detract us and distract us from going to the Lord. The world pulls us in many directions.

Go to a quiet space today. Sit comfortably and take three deep breaths slowly. Be filled with His breath of life. As your heart and mind draw near to Him, He draws near to you. God has been waiting for you to come to Him just as you are.

In yesterday's devotional, you may have become more aware of the things your soul thirsts for. Today, ask the Holy Spirit to reveal to you the different sources you go to for relief from anxiety, for comfort from the inner struggles within you, or to fill your emotional needs apart from God.

Share with your Heavenly Father whatever came to mind regarding the things you go to for comfort aside from Him.

Ask God for forgiveness for going to those wells and not always seeking His Living Water first.

Allow His compassion and grace to touch your heart. He welcomes you into His Presence, which is more than enough. Receive His peace. Ask the Lord to share His heart with you today and journal His messages to you.

FINALLY FULFILLED

Writing by Brittni De La Mora

I had blonde hair and braces. I was terrified as I spun around the pole at the strip club in Mexico for the first time at the age of 16. "What am I doing? How did I end up here?" I thought. Life had taken a sudden turn, but as I heard the applause of people cheering me on as I took my shirt off, I thought I had finally found what my soul had been hungering for…affirmation.

Growing up in my household I never heard the words, "I am proud of you. I love you. You're doing an amazing job." I was a straight A-student, I should have heard those words. Instead I heard, "I hate you! I wish you were never born. You're a loser." These words broke me of all courage and robbed me of my confidence. I didn't know who I was nor what I was purposed for on this earth. The day I realized my life had no real meaning was the day my search began. I knew I wanted to find love, but I had no idea what that even looked like, nor where to find it.

After jumping from man to man ending in heartbreak after heartbreak, I ended up in the strip club. That night I received so much affirmation, I thought I had finally found my purpose in life. I also thought I had found real true love. Never in my life had I been more affirmed than I was that night in the strip club. The affirmation made me feel like I finally belonged somewhere, I didn't feel like a reject in the strip club. I felt wanted. At 18-years old, the strip club led me into the adult film industry where I was named one of the world's hottest porn stars. However, something was still missing. Suddenly, what once fed my hunger now left me hungry. Affirmation was no longer enough to feed my soul. I needed something more, something greater than myself.

I imagine this must be how the Samaritan woman must have felt prior to encountering Jesus at the well. After five failed marriages and having a live-in boyfriend, it is clear to me she was looking for love in all the wrong places. Like me, she was feeding her soul with what was never designed to feed it. Like the Samaritan woman, Jesus came to my rescue. He fed me everything I had

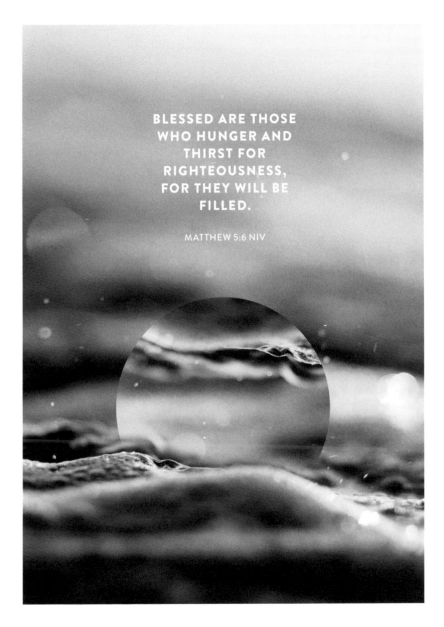

BLESSED ARE THOSE WHO HUNGER AND THIRST FOR RIGHTEOUSNESS, FOR THEY WILL BE FILLED.

MATTHEW 5:6 NIV

ever hungered for. He showed me a love so deep, it made every other ounce of love I had ever received appear so shallow.

When we hunger and thirst for God, it is then and only then we will be filled. When the woman at the well encountered Jesus, her life was forever changed. She was fed living water that created life within her.

Prayer

"Father, I want to encounter you like the woman at the well did. I have been feeding on things that have not satisfied my soul. I recognize only you can do that. I pray you will lead me into a place where I can feel satisfied with and full of your presence. I surrender my will and I give you my life. In Jesus name, Amen."

Challenge

This journey through these 21 days is about God pursuing you and your response to His invitation to draw near to Him and open your heart to all He has to give you. Will you give Him permission to take you deeper into His love for you? Journal your reflections.

When possible, find a quiet place and lie down or sit in a comfortable position. Listen to the worship song, "Reckless Love of God" by Cory Asbury. Allow the words to soak into you and rest in God's Presence.

Like nagging pain or a fever that never
subsides, shame torments, distracts,
steals joy and diverts us from our
God-given destiny and purpose. We may
be able to survive but we won't thrive with
the affliction of shame. In this section,
open your heart to encounter The One who
heals the brokenhearted with grace that
releases you to walk in freedom.

———

/healing shame_

When I think back to that moment, my skin still crawls, and the memory gnaws painfully at my soul when recalling the details. The sights, the sounds, the all-consuming fear. My arms printed raw with mahogany bruises, marks from where he held me down. My throat tight from sobbing, my heart burning with hatred and despair, my mind wracked with unrelenting fear. The bed sheets soaked with that awful scarlet red, evidence of my stolen innocence, and a reminder of his violent profession of love.

Love? How could that be love? Sick, twisted. He claimed to love me, yet after he raped me, he hated me. Left me feeling worthless. Left me believing that it was my fault. Left me alone, but even worse, he left me feeling abandoned. Abandonment birthed within me this unexplainable shame, leaving me to be tortured by these thoughts of "What if I had…" or "If only I hadn't…" I was marked as worthless. I was known to many after this violation as the 'desolate woman.'

As I reflect on those lonely days I spent, God was my only source of strength and hope to press through each moment He was my source of promise that someday I would behold Him face to face, that someday He would restore my soul and make me whole.

Some people allow their pain to define them, trapping them in a world of bitterness, isolating them from freedom, joy and love—the ability to love and to be loved. I am too familiar with such feelings.

Though I lived in shame for the rest of my earthly life, you do not have to! You, Beloved, are so blessed to live in a time in history where streams of healing flow from heaven through God breathed ministries that have received keys to healing the heart. My culture and time did not provide such pathways. The Holy Spirit has been given to comfort, heal, and transform your life!

My heart bursts with excitement as I shout out to you, "Pursue your healing! Become a Brave-Heart and journey wherever God would take you. He is able to restore. God's love contends for your breakthrough. You are marked by His love!"

His love never fails…

RESTORED

Writing by Karla Sumner

What do you remember when you were seven years old? Was it learning to ride a bike or learning to read? It was different for me. I was raised in a Christian home. My father was a pastor. Whenever my parents would go on ministry trips, they would have me stay at friends' homes.

One night, while my parents were away on one of their trips, my friend's older sister came into the room when I was alone. She locked the door. Silence filled the room as she began to tell me what she would 'do to me sexually' and what 'I would do to her sexually.' I was so confused! Fear gripped me as I tried to process what she was saying. I did what she told me to do. This trauma caused my whole world to change. Shame entered my heart. I began to hide and clothe myself in shame.

It wasn't long before I ran into another situation that reinforced my shame as a teenager. One Friday night, I decided to hang out with a boy that I had started talking to on social media. "I can't believe he wants to hang out with me," I thought with excitement. Although something deep down inside told me to run, I stubbornly went.

As he reached out to grab my hand, he led me down the beach from the party we were at. He began to kiss me and tell me that I was beautiful. My heart started to race. Suddenly, he began tearing off my clothes. Everything happened so fast. "Is he doing what I think he's doing?" I thought as he pushed me down. Forcing himself upon me, I screamed, "No! Please stop!" But he wouldn't! It was so painful and confusing. I was raped that night. Shame overwhelmed me, and thoughts tormented me, "Was this my fault? Did I deserve this? Is God as disgusted with me as I am with myself? I am such a wreck!" I felt so alone and powerless.

It wasn't until I finally decided to pursue God's healing, that I encountered God's reckless love that captured my heart. As I ran into the arms of Jesus,

"He showed me a picture of my wounded heart covered with band-aids. It had become infected because I didn't know how to clean it correctly. His perfect love cast out my fears and restored my heart."

He showed me a picture of my wounded heart covered with band-aids. It had become infected because I didn't know how to clean it correctly. His perfect love cast out my fears and restored my heart.

Jesus wants your mess—no matter how small or huge you believe your mess is. Shame can enter your life from a variety of ways. We all can struggle with varying levels of shame from not performing perfectly, from our failures or wrong choices, or from hurtful things said or done to us. He longs to heal us of our broken ways of coping.

In Him there is joy, freedom, and pure love for you! There is forgiveness for yourself and others! You have a voice that deserves to be heard. Beloved, do not push His love away, as I did for many years, but open your heart today to receive His unending grace and love for you.

Prayer

"Dear Father, thank you for never giving up on me. Thank you for your relentless love that fights for me. Give me the grace to allow you into the deepest parts of my heart. Give me your eyes to see how you see. I ask that your perfect love fill me. I give you permission to rip the band-aids of shame off my heart! I trust that you will complete the beautiful, brilliant work that you started in me. I love you!"

Challenge

Go to a private place that has a mirror. Stand tall and strong with good posture. Look at yourself in the mirror. Look deeply into your eyes and declare:

"I forgive myself!
I choose, with God's strength, to forgive those that hurt me.
I love myself because I am God's treasure.
God's perfect love casts out fear in me!
I am IMMENSELY loved by God!
I receive all the love and goodness God has for me today!
I have incredible value!
I am His beloved child who trusts in Him.
God is my safe place!"

Journal your reflections.

Another key to healing and freedom is forgiving those who have hurt you. Forgiveness is a process, especially if it is related to a traumatic experience.

As part of the healing process, what can be helpful is to get all your raw, unfiltered emotions and thoughts on paper regarding your experience in the form of a letter to the person who hurt you—a letter that would never actually be sent. God understands and already knows how you feel completely. In this letter, you would express everything you feel and think honestly towards him/her. After you write this letter, tear it up completely and throw it away. Seal that moment by praying something like, "Lord, I give this all to you!" Writing this letter would be a way of releasing your pain to the Lord.

After tearing up and throwing away this first letter, write a second letter to the Lord. Express your forgiveness toward the person who hurt you (or ask God to help you to forgive), ask God to forgive you for your unforgiveness, and even write a prayer of blessing for the person who hurt you. This may be a painful process, but forgiveness is a pathway worth beginning and pursuing to thrive and mature in Christ.

If you are having difficulty forgiving yourself or others, ask for help from spiritually mature people in your life. Support from others is necessary, especially when processing through a deep hurt.

THE GREAT EXCHANGE

Writing by Mikela Kobayashi

I knew all the statistics about sexually transmitted infections, teen pregnancy, and contraceptives. However, no one prepared me for the emotional damage that accompanied sex before marriage.

I was a sophomore in high school when I got into my first relationship. He was kind and funny, so naturally I was attracted to him. Several months into our relationship, we started becoming more physical. At the same time, the older girls in my dance classes would tell stories about what they did with their boyfriends and encouraged me that as long as I loved my boyfriend, it was okay to adventure further.

So, we did.

What those girls did not prepare me for was the amount of jealousy, self-doubt, and attachment that would come with giving up my virginity. Then, it got worse. One morning during my senior year, I was chatting with my girlfriends before school when I got the news that my boyfriend had been sleeping with another girl! At that moment, I lost all self-control and let my whole world crumble to the ground. I had never felt such intense pain, anger, or betrayal.

For years afterwards, I would look into the mirror and see someone who was inadequate, forgotten, slutty, damaged goods, and unwanted. Yet my heart was still so desperate to be loved.

As I entered into my first years of college, I also entered into new relationships. Except this time, I developed friendships with faithful young women who genuinely loved Jesus. Being around these women challenged me to meet this Jesus they loved so much. Once I let Jesus into my heart, I was conflicted with a choice to either continue to live by my hopeless identity and lifestyle or to plunge 100% into a life with Jesus. I remember the moment I sat in my green Honda Civic with tears flooding from my eyes, crying out to Jesus saying, "I don't want to live a double life anymore! I want You, Jesus!"

As I took a step towards Jesus, I also took a step towards vulnerability and healing. I let Jesus come into the deepest, most embarrassing parts of my heart so He could heal it. On this journey of healing, I traded the attributes I believed about myself for the truth of who He said I was. I traded inadequate for worthy. Forgotten for important. Slutty for pure. Damaged goods for beauty. Unwanted for loved much.

You too can make this trade. I want you to know, there is nothing that is unforgivable. There's no secret too deep, no lie too heavy, no fear too powerful that Jesus cannot heal and restore. Take a step towards Jesus. Trust Him. Make the great exchange.

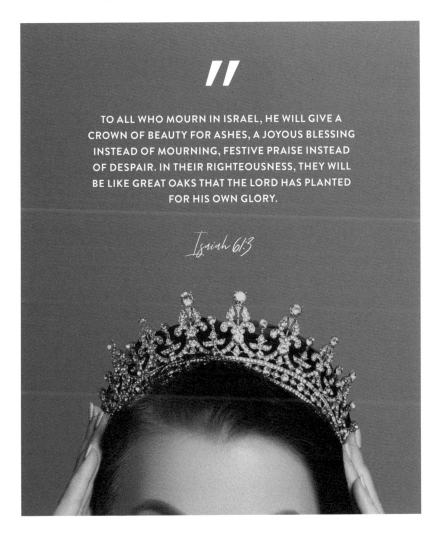

TO ALL WHO MOURN IN ISRAEL, HE WILL GIVE A CROWN OF BEAUTY FOR ASHES, A JOYOUS BLESSING INSTEAD OF MOURNING, FESTIVE PRAISE INSTEAD OF DESPAIR. IN THEIR RIGHTEOUSNESS, THEY WILL BE LIKE GREAT OAKS THAT THE LORD HAS PLANTED FOR HIS OWN GLORY.

Isaiah 61:3

"To all who mourn in Israel, he will give a crown of beauty for ashes, a joyous blessing instead of mourning, Festive praise instead of despair. In their righteousness, they will be like great oaks that the Lord has planted for his own glory." Isaiah 61:3 NLT

Challenge
On a piece of paper, write the word, "lies." Have a vulnerable moment with God and ask Him, "God, what are the negative lies that I believe about myself?" Allow Him to bring to light a few lies that you've believed and write them on the paper.

After writing your lies, go over each lie and declare,
"Father I break the lie _____ !"

When done, pray, "Father, I release these lies that I've believed in exchange for Your truth." Crumple and throw this paper away.

Remember, God is always gracious and never condescending. Now ask Him this very important follow up question, "What is the truth of how you see me?" Meditate on His truths. Journal your reflections.

If you can, listen to the song, "Speak to Me" by Kari Jobe before you journal. (Otherwise, plan a time to listen to this song.) Allow God to speak to you during this meditative time.

HOPE AND HEALING

Writing by Edward Sariol

Growing up, I was used to people calling me gay. Bullies in school would constantly harass me and make me cry. At family events, the word 'bakla' (the Filipino word for gay) would commonly be thrown around in conversations with me as the subject. Despite my effeminate demeanor and my best efforts to be caring toward others, it seemed the verdict of my life was already decided, and I just needed to accept it. Was I gay? Why do I have these feelings towards other guys? I would cry out in prayer, "God please take these feelings away from me!" Somehow in my Catholic upbringing, I knew the Bible said that homosexuality is wrong, but how do I reconcile my faith with my feelings? Moving forward, I stuffed away my attraction toward men and tried to act as straight and manly as possible.

In the 10th grade, I started attending church, a place where I didn't feel judged. Church family members didn't treat me differently from other guys. I wasn't 'gay' to them, I was a young man worthy of respect and dignity. As I grew in my faith, I discovered God's love and His desire for a relationship with me…I was sold! I committed my life to Him. I enjoyed serving in many church ministries, but the struggle inside me remained.

Over time, I realized I couldn't deny my inner struggle any longer. I decided to 'come out' to my pastor, because I was so full of shame and guilt. I didn't want to live a double life of serving God and battling with such feelings anymore.

My pastor is a man's man. He's tall and buff, likes to lift weights, plays football, basketball, boxing, and enjoys MMA fighting. A complete opposite of me! I was nervous about how he would respond to my confession. I expected him to hate me and kick me out of church. I thought, "I'll just tell him quick, and then bow out gracefully forever."

His response shocked me. He gently responded, "Ok, we're gonna work it out."

At first, I was confused. I thought, "How can we work this out? Like it's an actual workable situation?!" Yet, in that moment, I was also freed from the shackles of shame. My vulnerability was met with God's kindness, grace, and hope through my pastor.

God used that moment to start me on a great journey of healing, freedom, and miracles of the heart. He has since taught me the truth of who a godly man really is and how He created me to be. I learned to forgive the people who had hurt me, including my parents. God empowered me to reject the lies and labels that others had tried to put on me while growing up. I also learned who I really am in Christ, that my value and identity is in Him and in the truth of His Word alone!

A key breakthrough moment from my shame was when I confided my story and struggle with my pastor. He would say of secret struggles, "It's like a cavity; you can only hide it for so long. It'll just keep eating you up inside and cause you pain until you open up and tell someone about it."

Whatever your struggle is, I encourage you, God offers you healing, hope and the answers you are seeking!

Challenge

Whether you struggle with same-sex temptation or not, you are not alone in your battles. The Christian life is full of all kinds of struggles, pain, trials, and challenges. And it is also a life full of promise, purpose, victories, hope, joy, peace, miracles, and glorious encounters with God's healing love and power. Beloved, we are all in the process of growing, maturing, and transforming into Christ's image. The Lord is committed to be a faithful, ever-present, understanding, patient, and compassionate God who is for you.

There is also great protection and support for you as you live in community with other followers of Christ. God will often minister through His people. I encourage you to talk openly with your pastor or spiritual leader. Find other godly brothers and sisters to walk alongside you in your healing journey with the Lord. It is difficult for shame to have a grip on you when you tangibly experience the unconditional love and grace from God's people. You can also receive healing as you invite prayer support from others. Your transformation process might not look perfect but allow God to guide you through being confident that He will complete the good work He has started in you!

"Confess your sins to each other and pray for each other so that you may be healed. The earnest prayer of a righteous person has great power and produces wonderful results." James 5:16 NLT

Meditate on Philippians 1:6 below. Allow God to encourage your heart, knowing He is faithful to transform you as you seek Him. Journal what you sense God is speaking to your heart.

"*I pray with great faith for you*, because I'm fully convinced that the One who began this glorious work in you will faithfully continue the process of maturing you and will put his finishing touches to it until the unveiling of our Lord Jesus Christ!" Philippians 1:6 TPT

FREEDOM

Writing by Louisa Wendorff

Even after singing at the Grammy Awards…or receiving support and affirmation by mega star Taylor Swift… looking put together on the outside and experiencing moments of fame as a singer/song-writer…the world did not have a clue about my inner world at the time. Yet, God was at work wooing me closer to His Heart.

Hear my journey

—

Feeling higher, lower, smaller, bigger;
fighting longer and longer the struggle never ended.
Surrounded by nothing but competition, expectation, comparison and pressure.
Pressure to succeed in everyone else's eyes, in every area of my life.

I broke under the pressure again and again, with only moments of temporary relief.
I couldn't get out from under the control and mental torment of never being enough.
I believed I needed to meet this expectation to be worth something.

I did it! I looked perfect from head to toe with a smile that convinced everyone including myself I was okay.
But the reality was, I was desperate.
Desperate for love, for identity, starving myself most days, covering up the pain of mental, emotional, and sexual abuse, all to maintain this false perception of perfection.

I was alone, bound to this sin-cycle, addiction of people-pleasing and self-hatred, keeping me stuck in shame.
It was hollow, dark, empty, oppressive.
But fear locked me in so tight that I almost didn't want to get out, not fully at least.
I wanted to maintain control to some point.
The fact was, I didn't trust God, I didn't trust His love for me, His plan, the power of the blood of Jesus.
I thought I "believed" it my whole life, but my heart and my life were proving my unbelief.

I didn't even know I didn't trust Him!
Not until I encountered the tangible, powerful, healing Love of the Father.
It beckoned me in my brokenness.
He asked me to trade my trash for his treasure.
My fear, control, constant anxiety, sickness;
For His peace, His love, His healing, His mercy.
An uneven trade paid for long, long ago, to give us LIFE and FREEDOM when
we didn't deserve it.
Choose His love and power to be Lord over your life; in every area.
Trust Him by fully letting go and allowing Him to be God.
Turn away and disconnect yourself from every lie that you've agreed with whether
you or someone else has spoken it over your life.
Refuse to believe anything but the Truth!
You are loved.
Freedom has been purchased for you!
Jesus has already won this war!

"I sought the Lord, and he answered me; he delivered me from all my fears. Those who look to him are radiant; their faces are never covered with shame." Psalm 34:4-5 NIV

Challenge

God longs to free you from the chains of your shame, whether it's regarding body image, a drive to please people, or lingering unhealed wounds in your heart.

Find a quiet place and listen to the song "Glorious Day" by Passion. Meditate on the words—this can be a reality for you today!

There is great power in your spoken word. Declare each of these statements slowly and deliberately, pausing after each phrase. Allow the Lord to touch you.

"The heart of God is burning with passion for me.
My worth does not alter. Ever.
Jesus dying on the cross is proof for His love for me.
I am not a disappointment, I am His shining treasure!
He wants me for me.
Not for my gifts and talents, or works, nor for my looks or accomplishments.
He wants my eyes. He wants my WHOLE heart.
He desires me.
God is my best friend, my defender, my counselor.
He is my loving Father and lover of my soul!"

Journal what God is highlighting to you today from today's message.

FINDING HOME

Writing by Joshua Ko

"I have no friends..." Have you ever said that to yourself? These were the words and the feelings that I felt and expressed after coming home from a rough day at school. High school for me was difficult. Most of my closest friends had changed schools in the transition from middle school to high school, and the "friends" that remained at my school were getting into relationships. Just because there were many classmates around, it didn't mean that they were all my friends. How could I be surrounded by so many people, yet still feel so alone?

Have you ever felt that way—the feeling of being around people, but not having deep connection? While you may have many 'friends' on Facebook, or followers on Instagram, and snaps on Snapchat, there is still a deep desire for something more than just the superficial. It may seem like everyone is there for the main events of your life, but when it comes to the daily, or even the painful moments, everyone is gone. The reality is, we were created to have connection and community.

From the very beginning, God said that everything He created was good. From the highest peak of the mountains to the fish who dwelt in the depths, God saw all He created and said it was good...except one thing. God saw Adam alone, and saw that it was not good. He then created a companion, a friend, and helper, to be by his side to carry on in life.

We were not created to be alone, but to have a home. Sin has its way of putting up walls, so God sent Jesus to tear down sin, prejudice, and racism to create a new community based on transparency and unconditional love. I learned that when Christ lives in me, there is no room for judgment.

The one thing that everyone shares in common is suffering, and the relationships that are true are those who like Christ, will endure through your deepest pain. While there were many people around me during my high school season, I was the one who was not comfortable with people seeing me struggle. Although risky, I found that when you open up to people, they will tend to feel the liberty to do the same with you.

During my senior year, I found a true friend who later became my best friend—not because we had many things in common, but because we were both able to share our struggles openly and honestly. We didn't judge each other, we listened, understood, and encouraged each other. Shame free zone.

God's love heals shame, restores, gives joy, value, and purpose. An important way we encounter God's love is through people, through a loving community. In 'family,' God desires for us to experience acceptance and unconditional love despite whatever we have gone through in life. Relationships where we can tangibly experience His grace. This is God's heart for you!

"To the fatherless he is a father. To the widow he is a champion friend. To the lonely he gives a family…" Psalm 68:5-6 TPT

Prayer

"Father, I was created to connect with others. As I create connection and community with others, fill me with joy overflowing and a sense of purpose, satisfying my need for connection. Bring me friends who I can share your love with and friends that would encourage me to run after you. Amen."

Challenge

We are all children…each with a heart that longs to find home. This is a God-given desire.

First, we must find our home in God:

(Jesus said) "Live in me. Make your home in me just as I do in you." John 15:4 MSG

We also are called to find a home in the family of God.

In hindsight, looking back at my high school years, there were many opportunities for me to connect with others and live in community. I want to challenge you to not remain alone but to seek for a Christ-centered, life-giving community that will encourage you to really live in freedom from shame! It could be a church, youth group, or some small group. Be a safe place for others to be open and open yourself to them.

If you do not currently have close friends that encourage you in your walk with God, ask the Lord to provide.

If you are not currently part of a loving community of God's people, pray for his direction and provision. Take steps to find a home.

If you have close friends and are planted in a loving Christian community, pray for a deeper connection with the people in your life and reach out to those you notice who need a home, as God leads you.

Journal a prayer to the Lord.

Love verses lust. Selfish verses selfless.
Quite a tug of war. A roving eye, a search for
sensual pleasures in a person, object or source
of power—these are common to all.
C.S. Lewis said, "Love is the great conqueror
of lust," and God is love. In this section,
experience real-life snapshots of this relentless
love at work—a love that can woo you out
from any dark shadow into a glorious light
that makes all things new.

———

/victorious love_

"A man after God's own heart." That's how I'm usually described. Righteous. Wise. Perfect, right? No. There's only one King that fits that description, and it certainly isn't me.

I had my moments, sure! I spared Saul's life when I could have killed him and become king. I danced for God with all my might when they brought back the Ark of the Covenant. I wrote almost half the book of Psalms.

But, did you know I had a problem with lust?

One of my greatest failures—of which there were many, I promise you—was when I saw a woman taking a bath on her roof. I could have walked away, closed the window, or just looked away! I didn't. I watched.

One choice! One foolish, tiny lapse of judgment. Because of that choice, I kept choosing sin for a while. I called this woman to my bedroom. I used my power and authority as king, to convince her to sleep with me. She got pregnant,

then I tried to cover it up. I even had her husband killed to hide my guilt.

You see, lust is concerned with what you can get for yourself. Love honors and benefits others.

My lust, and the shame that followed would have swallowed me up if it wasn't for God's grace and kindness. He sent the prophet Nathan, my friend, to call out my denial to my face. I endured the painful consequences of my actions. Weeping bitterly, I asked God to forgive me, and put me back on His path.

Repentance—turning from my way to God's way. That's what made me "a man after God's own heart." I wanted God to be glorified in my life. His kindness kept leading me away from lust, away from my brokenness, and back to Him.

Not perfection, but passion. God is not asking you to be perfect, but to passionately seek him. Honoring Him and submitting to His pure and loving way brings the joy, blessing, and life you seek. He wanted my heart and He wants yours too.

✖

A a creative narrative written by John Allison based on David found in I Samuel 11 and 12:1-22

CHOOSING LOVE

Writing by Derek Devine

My teammate, who owned a strip club, invited me to this event. There I was, at my first National Football League party—something I always heard about but never experienced. Gorgeous women were literally flown in for this event.

I had reached the pinnacle of my athletic career. I had just signed a 3-year contract with the Seattle Seahawks. I had finally accomplished a dream that I had been chasing since I was 5 years old. I had no room to focus on anything else. However, what I never really considered until I got to the NFL, was what was I going to do when the lifestyle of the NFL challenged my faith?

From the moment I walked into the room, women were throwing themselves at me. These women kept inviting me to go with them to a downstairs bedroom. My teammate urged me, "Come on man! Go down there with the women so they can take care of you."

Love or lust. Lust is self-centered. Love puts the welfare of others first. Which would I choose? My example would mean nothing to my teammates if I made the choice to lust in that moment. The battle in my mind and heart was real.

Mustering up courage, I replied to my teammate, "I appreciate your thought, but that is not who I am." He stood shocked at my response. He had NEVER seen a man deny himself as I just did.

"Why man?" He asked me.

I shared with him about my relationship with Jesus—how He gave me the life and love that I longed for. I was able to plant a seed of faith that was demonstrated to my friend in a real-life moment. Eyes were watching me, and the accountability that gave me, helped me to choose rightly.

We can face situations in life where giving into our sexual desires in the moment is literally a battle. Giving into lust can lead us to so many dark places. Lust can rob

LOVE IS THE MARK...

OF TRUE MATURITY.

us of our destiny and destroy our lives and relationships. Whether it is watching porn to choosing to dwell on fantasies…the struggle is real. Temptations will come our way.

Our hearts can lust for many things—power, money, the list can go on. What kind of lusts do you wrestle with? You are not alone. God cares and desires to walk with you into victory when the battle is hot. If you have given into lust, know there is grace, healing and forgiveness in God. Bring your burdens to God and find those who can give you the accountability that can strengthen and guide you!

"You are always and dearly loved by God! So robe yourself with virtues of God, since you have been divinely chosen to be holy. Be merciful as you endeavor to understand others, and be compassionate, showing kindness toward all. Be gentle and humble, unoffendable in your patience with others. Tolerate the weaknesses of those in the family of faith, forgiving one another in the same way you have been graciously forgiven by Jesus Christ. If you find fault with someone, release this same gift of forgiveness to them. For **love is supreme** and must flow through each of these virtues. **Love becomes the mark of true maturity.**" Colossians 3:12-13 TPT, bold added

Challenge

To love is a choice—it requires effort, focus, determination, and sacrifice. I propose to you, instead of giving in to lust, no matter what kind of lust, let's focus on loving.

Having a plan for what you would do in moments of temptation can be a great help. Take some time and figure out what action steps would help you to get into a place of victory. Consider having some of your close friends join in and support you on that plan.

God has a great plan for your life that may very well include marriage. If you desire to be married someday, you can journal a prayer to the Lord about your hopes and dreams for a future spouse and family. In this prayer, consider including a commitment to grow in Christ and in His character, to learn how to have healthy, godly, relationships, and to walk in sexual integrity. All these efforts will support and build a strong foundation for your future, including a firm foundation for a marriage and family!

Before journaling your reflections, spend a few moments in prayer and get in touch with your dreams, hopes, and your heart's desire for an amazing future.

Day 10

INTO THE LIGHT

Writing by Brandon Ahu

"No one can ever know about this," I vowed to my teenage self as I hid the porn magazine under my bed, far from unintended eyes. A strange blend of shame, arousal, and secrecy swirled through my mind as I tried to balance what I knew was wrong with what my untamed sexuality craved.

Hidden magazines soon mutated to the horrible Pandora's box of online pornography, and I soon found myself enslaved to my secret addiction—one that I wanted NO ONE to find out about.

Whenever people were going to come over to our house, my mom would make me clean my room. But rather than spend time to actually put things away neatly, throw trash out, and sort through my belongings, I would just do the most convenient option—stuff it all in my closet. Problem solved. Just don't look in there. I would have put a giant "Keep Out!" sign on my closet if I could.

But while that may have worked a few times, the stench of unwashed gym clothes, damp surf shorts, and forgotten about food eventually created a cocktail of smells that rivaled the local dump. So, it is with hidden sin. Rather than deal with our mistakes, failures, and shame-filled addictions, we often just push it all into a closet that no one is allowed to look in. Because if anyone ever looked in there, their opinion of you might change, right? Because whatever you're hiding doesn't really have a hold on you since you can quit anytime, right? Because you can beat this on your own, right?

Wrong.

Wrestling with hidden sin is a losing battle. It's impossible to beat an enemy that we don't admit actually exists. For so many of us, it's easier to push our struggles into unspoken secrecy than to actually confront them. But eventually, it all comes out into the light. You can be vulnerable with God—He longs to be your safe place. Hear Him beckoning you out of your closet of shame. He cares passionately for you and desires to free you and lead you. It is your time to allow God's healing and cleansing light into the areas we hide in. Let courage rise within you to bring it all into the light and let Jesus set you free from what has kept you enslaved!

"God, I invite your searching gaze into my heart.
Examine me through and through;
Find out everything
That may be hidden within me.
Put me to the test, and sift through
All my anxious cares.
See if there is any path of pain I'm walking on,
And lead me back to your glorious, everlasting ways,
The path that brings me back to you."
Psalm 139:23-24 TPT

Challenge

In a quiet space, give the Lord permission to search your heart with His healing light and reveal the things you hide from Him—and even from yourself.

Confess those things to Him in prayer and invite Him to help you to make your path straight once again.

Make a short list of a few people you trust and feel safe to be vulnerable with. Write the names of those that come to mind on the blanks below:

(If you can't think of anyone, then that can be a prayer of yours—for God to highlight someone in your life that can become that safe person.)

_____

_____

Confide at least one of your struggles to a trusted friend, mentor, parent, spiritual mom, spiritual dad, or pastor that came to your mind. Ask them for prayer and for help. This can be the start of breakthrough, freedom, and healing for you in these areas!

Ask the Lord to share with you His thoughts toward you today. Begin your journal with "Dear (*your name*)" and journal a letter from God to you, writing down His encouraging words that come to mind.

PURE

Writing by Richie Cruz

There I was…a six-year-old boy innocently playing with my classmates on the playground. A friend called me towards him near a secluded area of the schoolyard. He wanted to show me something. Curious, I went to him excited to see what he wanted to show me. "Here's a picture of a naked lady." He shoved a ripped-out magazine photo of a completely naked woman in front of me. Instantly, I felt embarrassed and excited at the same time. Something new was happening within me as my eyes locked onto the image. It felt like what we were looking at was bad and that at any moment we would be caught and sent to the office with a phone call to our parents. To our relief, none of those consequences happened. However, years later that event would haunt me and drastically affect my life, my relationships, and the way I viewed sex and sexuality.

If I knew growing up what I know now regarding the harms of pornography, things would have been a whole lot different. I would have known that porn acts as a drug, rewiring and changing the brain the exact way that cocaine does. I would have known that the porn industry creates long-term customers by targeting young viewers. I would have known that human sex trafficking and porn are linked, and that porn creates a false, unhealthy view of sex. I would have known how lonely I would feel fighting my secret battle. And…I would have known that watching porn kills love and hurts the hearts of those closest to me.

Yet, even after experiencing these devastating effects of porn, God rescued me and set me free from this addiction! Yet I know myself enough and how important it is to keep on guard and accountable to others. It is a daily choice to walk in the light.

God is able to give you keys to fight and win this battle against porn! You don't have to damage your brain, hurt your relationships, or be alone. The Lord gladly gives you the power to say yes to purity and guard against the strategies of the enemy.

Are you stressed? Angry? Lonely? Need to feel in control? Feeling rejected? Are you weary of life's trials? Need to feel powerful? God desires to shine His healing light on the WHY behind what we do, and what drives us to any go-to addiction you may be struggling with.

If you don't struggle with porn, become a shame-free zone for others. Together, let's have brave hearts to contend for each other's freedom. There is hope and breakthrough!

The Lord is able to create in you a pure heart that calls down His favor and blessings upon your life!

"What bliss you experience when your heart is pure! For then your eyes will be open to see more and more of God." Matthew 5:8 TPT

Prayer

"Father, help me to resist the temptation to look at pornography (If you don't struggle with porn, name what you go to for comfort aside from God). Show me the way out of those times of temptation and give me the strength to choose the way of purity. Renew my mind to view sex the way YOU view it. I give you my eyes, my desires, my sexuality, my mind, and my heart. Give me courage to stay open and accountable to my spiritual family. Purify my heart that I may see you more!"

Challenge

If you struggle with porn, you can go to God to ask for forgiveness for this 'what,' but search your heart and ask God for forgiveness for the 'why' and for not turning to Him to fill that need.

Pursue your own healing and connect with someone who will not only hold you accountable but will speak courage and strength to you along the way.

Consider inviting the Lord into your struggle or addiction, whatever that may be. Ask Him to share with you His loving thoughts toward you and reveal to you the roots of how you got to where you are. He desires to walk with you to freedom, so you can live out of a pure heart and mind.

Journal any insights and encouragement that come to mind.

PLEASURE YOURSELF

Writing by Richie Cruz

When was the last time you experienced the pleasure and thrill of life? Was it going down a roller coaster at Disneyland? Seeing breathtaking scenery at the top of a mountain? Going surfing on that perfect wave? Did you know that God is the author of pleasure and wants you to experience His pleasure?

Pleasure has been around since the Garden of Eden (which means "Garden of Pleasure"). Pleasure was and is God's idea. We were created out of God's pleasure, for pleasure. God really wants His children to experience pleasure and to experience it regularly. However, It's the source of that pleasure that makes all the difference. Not all pleasure brings life.

Sin is pleasurable...for a time. We wouldn't do it if it didn't feel good. The result of sin, however, is not so much pleasurable. Broken relationships, broken trust, broken faith and broken hearts are usually the result of the "pleasures of sin." There was a time in my life that I used to think that watching porn and masturbating was a way to pleasure myself.

For some of us, masturbation is an addiction, or at least is something we turn to for comfort for that moment of fleeting pleasure. God's intention for sexual pleasure is connection with your spouse. Masturbation does not give us that intimacy, in fact, it can train our minds to move away from connection. Seek God's very best. God has a better way for us to pleasure ourselves that will always result in joy. And it's only found in His Presence.

"YOU MAKE KNOWN TO ME
THE PATH OF LIFE; YOU WILL FILL ME WITH JOY
IN YOUR PRESENCE, WITH ETERNAL PLEASURES
AT YOUR RIGHT HAND."

PSALM 16:11 NIV

Prayer
"Father God, show me the 'eternal pleasures' that are at your right hand. Show me the things that you have in store for me that bring me pleasure…and life. Help me to see how the 'pleasure of sin' harm and hurt myself and others. Teach me to pleasure myself with Your presence as I do the things that you created me to do."

Challenge
Reflect on the things that give you pleasure that are not harmful or negative but enhance your life positively.

Make a list here of your top three pleasures you are aware of:

This week, intentionally pursue those *healthy* pleasures and purpose to integrate these pleasures into your life.

In your journal today, ask the Lord to recall a moment when you experienced joy and pleasure (even a sense of fun) doing a meaningful activity in your life. Maybe it was creating an art piece, hiking, snowboarding, spending time at a café with good friends, or watching a sunset.

Journal that experience. How did you feel? What did you especially appreciate about that time? Ask the Lord what He thinks about that time.

LET LOVE BE YOUR HIGHEST GOAL

Writing by Marion and Charis Logan

Charis: Don't worry, we've all been there. After a romantic date, even though certain physical/sexual boundaries were clarified and in place, you push the limits. In the moment, it feels so right and sometimes the guilt doesn't come right away, but eventually it does. Ladies, you know what I mean right?

Marion: Guys, have you ever been in the heat of the moment and she was saying 'yes' 'yes' 'yes' to physically pushing the boundaries, but the next day something was not right?

Charis: When Marion and I were dating, we had a pattern. That exact scenario would happen. The next morning after "pushing it," I'd wake up and feel terrible and then take it out on him! I would feel so mad at him for not stopping and he was left feeling confused and upset because he didn't understand why I didn't say anything when we were "in the moment." I would lose respect for him and pull away. In turn he would withdraw his love from me.

It was by the grace of God and with the help of a few close, supportive people that we were very honest with, that Marion and I did not have sex before we got married.

Marion: When I think of respect, I associate it with leadership. Good leaders think ahead, make good decisions, think about others involved, and move at the right time. My then girlfriend's desire to please me drowned out her emotions of restraint and when her emotions came back, she was hurt and angry at me for not taking leadership. I failed as a leader because I was thinking of myself first—great leadership requires self-sacrifice. Charis always says, "A girl may be saying, 'Yes, yes, yes!' in the moment of passion, but she is hoping he will take leadership and say, 'No, no, no!' because he values her for more than just her body."

Charis: Even when it doesn't make sense, if we choose to love one another, especially in our dating relationship, we won't miss out on the things that make for a great relationship—love and respect. When we push it physically, the very thing we both long for is jeopardized. It may not seem to connect, but it always does. Let love be your highest goal!

"Love is large and incredibly patient. Love is gentle and consistently kind to all. It refuses to be jealous when blessing comes to someone else. Love does not brag about one's achievements nor inflate its own importance. Love does not traffic in shame and disrespect, nor selfishly seek its own honor. Love is not easily irritated or quick to take offense. Love joyfully celebrates honesty and finds no delight in what is wrong. Love is a safe place of shelter, for it never stops believing the best for others. Love never takes failure as defeat, for it never gives up." I Corinthians 13:4-7 TPT

Challenge

If you are in a dating relationship right now, please have a candid conversation with your significant other about the physical boundaries you want to establish and bring others into your lives to help keep you both accountable.

If you have pushed the limits in your relationship, take time to ask for forgiveness from one another. Ask the Lord to forgive you as well.

Bless each other in prayer as often as possible! If you can strengthen your spiritual connection with each other, this can greatly help each of you to be 'Spirit-led' in your decisions.

What is also very important, is to come up with a plan with how you will handle your time together (i.e. talk to mentors, be accountable, be specific in your boundaries).

If you are currently not in a dating relationship, you can still be preparing yourself for when you are in a relationship. Discover what are the healthiest boundaries you can have when you date. Let your values and vision guide your plan.

Journal any thoughts that were triggered within you as you read today's message. You can write a prayer and any messages from the Lord.

Which aspects of God are the easiest for you
to embrace in your heart? Which aspects
are the most difficult? Jesus came to reveal
the Father so the world would know His
passionate, forgiving heart of love. Read on
and grow in trusting your Heavenly Father's
wisdom and life-changing love for you.

———

/Father's heart_

We were old enough to be great-grandparents. I was 85 years old and my wife Sarah was 75. God had said we were to be His chosen 'First Family' of many nations even though we had no children and there was no sign of a baby anytime soon. After years of waiting in frustration and growing desperation for God's promise to be fulfilled, we decided to take matters into our own hands. Sarah urged me to sleep with her woman servant, Hagar, so I did. Through her, we hoped to have the son we wanted.

To my great delight, Hagar did get pregnant, but I did not foresee the unrelenting drama that soon followed. Jealousy and conflict between Sarah and Hagar became a constant undercurrent that infected my home.

Nevertheless, my love for Ishmael grew as the years went by.

When I turned 99, God told me that Sarah would finally give birth to the son He promised us. This was an astounding promise to me, but with deep concern for Ishmael, I cried out, "If only Ishmael might live under your blessing!"

I was stunned at what happened next. God replied and said He would give me the desire of my heart by making Ishmael into a great nation! Even though Ishmael was conceived in my disobedience and sin, God was nevertheless going to bless him!

The following year, Sarah gave birth to our son Isaac, and it wasn't long thereafter that all the strife in my family came to a breaking point. Ishmael was still a youth when Sarah demanded that Hagar and Ishmael leave, never to come back. How my heart ached at the thought of being separated from Ishmael, but God in His kindness, reassured me that He would be with Ishmael as he grew up.

Have you ever wondered if God would forgive you for something you knowingly did that was wrong? God not only forgave me; He blessed me beyond what I deserved. Ever felt overlooked, unwanted, or displaced? Trust that the Father deeply loves you as He loved Ishmael. Take the journey of grace and truth into the Father's Heart.

✖

A creative narrative written by Robert Okimura based on Abraham found in Genesis 16, 17, 18:1-15, 21:8-20

Day 14

FATHER'S AFFIRMATION

Writing by Marion Logan

When I was in second grade, my friend Timothy and I loved to bust out windows in vacant houses, cuss, enter into people's property, and pick fights with other neighborhood boys. We were rascals who were up to a bunch of shenanigans… until we got caught by my Dad. Oh! He would NOT be happy with me. He would give me a spanking and would ground me for all the rascal stuff I did.

I believed, "I'm a bad son—he could never be proud of me. I let my dad down." Then one day, the extra-ordinary happened. I was in my room, grounded again. My dad approached me, got on his knees, stooped down to my eye level, and looked at me face to face. He said, "You are better than this—you are a Logan! Logans don't lie, cheat, steal, or damage other's property. Logans are honest, hard-working, faithful, and honoring. You are a Logan. You are my son—don't forget it!" My dad reminded me of who I was. I felt so secure and validated. A confidence and a determination rose up in me to be that person of character my dad was calling forth.

With all the no good I had been up to, he could have easily called me 'stupid', 'you punk kid', or 'worthless.' Instead, at one of the lowest points of my young life, he reminded me that I have a name, an identity, and a destiny.

There is a story of a lost son in Luke 15:11-32 who made a mess of his life and lost everything. When he came home, he did not even feel worthy to be his son and would have gladly accepted being a servant for his father. But this loving father ran toward his son, embraced him, and reminded him of his identity when he saw him in the distance coming home. The father affirmed his son and reminded him that he will never cease being his son.

"But the father said to his servants, 'Quick! Bring the best robe and put it on him. Put a ring on his finger and sandals on his feet. Bring the fattened calf and kill it. Let's have a feast and celebrate. For this son of mine was dead and is alive again; he was lost and is found.' So they began to celebrate." Luke 15:22-24 NIV

...WITH YOUR HAND OF LOVE UPON MY LIFE,
YOU IMPART A FATHER'S BLESSING TO ME.
THIS IS JUST TOO WONDERFUL, DEEP,
AND INCOMPREHENSIBLE! YOUR UNDERSTANDING
OF ME BRINGS ME WONDER AND STRENGTH.

PSALM 139:5-6 TPT

Our Father God looks at us after we've made some messes in our lives. Right at that time we believe He could never be proud of us—He shows up big time. You may feel like what you have done is unforgivable or feel an overwhelming sense of shame for what has happened in your life. But God is a good, kind, compassionate Father who loves you and reminds you that you have an honorable name, identity, and a powerful destiny.

"...With your hand of love upon my life, You impart a Father's blessing to me. This is just too wonderful, Deep, and incomprehensible! Your understanding of me brings me wonder and strength." Psalm 139:5-6 TPT

Prayer

"Father, help me know what it means to be your child. Teach me how to walk as your Beloved One. Even though I may feel like a waste or not worthy to be yours—you remind me of who I am. You remind me that I was created for great things. Lord help me walk as the person you have destined me to be. I am never too far gone to not be your beloved son/daughter. Help me encounter your love and know that I am yours."

Challenge

It may be difficult to know our identity from our Heavenly Father because of the influence of our earthly father. For example, if our earthly father was untrustworthy and dishonest, then it would naturally be difficult to trust our Heavenly Father. If our earthly father was absent, or abusive, it can be difficult to believe that God is our advocate, protector and there for us.

Some of us may feel we have a great father, and that is a blessing. People have different experiences with their fathers. No father is perfect and most often, we have mixed experiences of our father's love. We may feel affirmed and have a sense of identity in areas of our lives where we feel loved but feel inadequate and unloved in other areas. What was/is your experience with your earthly father?

List below some adjectives you would use to describe your earthly father:

Now, examine the words describing your father. Are there positive words that reflect your Heavenly Father? Give God thanks for any positive attributes of your earthly father. Are there negative words in your description leading you to forgive your earthly father for any failings? Also, ask God to forgive you for any negative judgements you placed upon your father. Ask God to renew your mind to receive the truth of who He is: your loving, perfect, Heavenly Father.

Ask the Lord, "What kind of a Father are you? What are your kind intentions towards me? Describe yourself to me." Journal what comes to mind.

GOOD FATHER

Writing by Justin Torrence

One of my best friends is a man named Peter. He's a loving husband and father, a talented musician, and a smart businessman. Although Peter grew up in church and was once a worship leader, he's currently atheist.

Years ago, when Peter's first marriage was falling apart, we would chat for hours. He had chronic insomnia, was heavily medicated for his many physical ailments, began self-medicating with alcohol, and was in and out of psychiatric care (mostly because of the meds). It was too much. Then it ended - his marriage and his walk with the Lord.

Fast-forward to 2015. Peter had since remarried and had two children. I had just returned from filming The Heart of Man and was back in my hometown where Peter lived. Throughout the years, we continued to stay closely connected on a regular basis. I, being a Christian, was always aware that the Lord may use me to speak to Peter in our conversations. And he did. But the Lord also used those times to speak to me.

I remember one such occasion. Peter had been away on a business trip and returned to his car he had left parked at the airport. Surprisingly, he found a beautiful wooden box atop his car hood at the airport parking lot. "What the @#^$?!", he said. I was getting a play by play since I happened to be on the phone with him. As Peter opened the box, he discovered an impressive set of kitchen knives!

Here's the beauty of the knives: Peter LOVES to cook. I immediately knew this was a gift from the Father to his Prodigal Son. Something that would make his heart come alive. A gift that spoke directly to his love of cooking. I was just about to blurt out, "You should praise the Lord for that," when the Holy Spirit stopped me.

The Lord spoke to my heart, "I don't give gifts to get praise. I give gifts because I love."

Later that same night, we sat together on his porch, talking as we often did. I shared with Peter what the Lord told me about the box of knives, that it was about His love for him. Peter had been so used to the false notion that God demanded perfection. But God loved Peter - even in his doubt.

While playing the character of the Prodigal in The Heart of Man, I had to continuously step into the depths of our fallen human nature. Always being reminded of the far places to which we all run. What I love about this film is that it constantly reminds me of the places in us about which God is not intimidated.

He is not scared of our doubt or perturbed by our fear. He is not disappointed in our questions or appalled at our brokenness. He knows all about you and looks at you with the loving eyes of a perfect Father who wants you to rest in his love for you. That night, Peter and I got a clearer glimpse of God's true heart and character. Perhaps one of the most profound revelations either of us had ever had. As we sat together it was a conversation filled with, "What if God is this good? What if?!" And He is my friends. Trust me, He is.

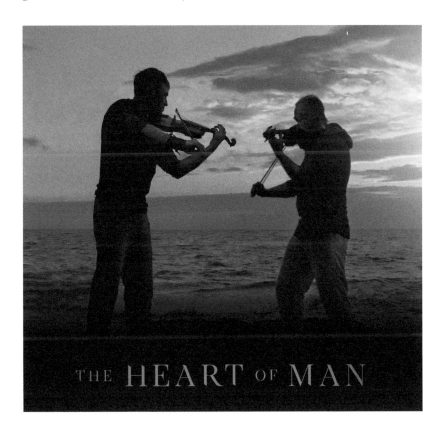

THE HEART OF MAN

"Look with wonder at the depth of the Father's marvelous love that he has lavished on us! He has called us and made us his very own beloved children..."
I John 3:1 TPT

Prayer
"Father, please reveal to me the depths of your love for me. Please reveal false beliefs that I have about who you are that do not align with your true Father's heart."

Examples of some false beliefs:

- You are waiting to punish me whenever I don't measure up.
- You are disappointed in me because I don't meet all your expectations.
- When I think of your expression, I see an angry, critical God judging me.
- I have long list of things I need to change about myself before you delight in me.
- I have to perform to earn your love.
- You don't really like me.

(Name any false beliefs that came to mind and/or any statements above that you identify with and surrender them to God.)

"Father, I give these false beliefs to you. I do not want them anymore! Remind me of the true Father's heart that you have towards ME. Thank you! Amen."

Challenge
Take a moment to think about a special positive memory you shared with your earthly father or a father figure in your life. Why was that memory memorable to you? How did it make you feel?

If you could paint a picture of a perfect father, what would he look like? How would he treat you and make you feel? Write down these thoughts. If you want, sketch a picture or write a poem that expresses your vision.

When you have an opportunity, get alone for a few moments. Quiet your thoughts and worries. Just breathe. Listen to the song, "Good, Good Father" sung by Housefires. Play it a few times if needed. Let the words wash over you.

TREASURE

Writing by Lea Hanashiro

I HATE MY RED, FRIZZY HAIR!!! This was the first thought I had every time I looked in the mirror. My perception was that the boys liked brown or blonde hair because my close friends all had boyfriends. So why would a boy ever look at me and say "Dang, she's fine!"? But that's what I wanted, I wanted boys to think that about me and ask me out. Then came college and I found myself just hoping I would catch someone's eye enough for them to come over and say hi, hopefully leading to a date.

Every time I would compare myself to another girl, there was always something I wanted to change about me. If you take this a little deeper, what you can see is that I was actually judging my own self! This led me down a road of fear, negativity, and self-hatred. My sexuality was being expressed through my lens of what I believed about myself. But what was I afraid of deep down? I was afraid of not being good enough for someone to love.

With the chaos going on around me, it was easy to have confusing and lonely thoughts of wondering where I fit and who I fit with in this world. I had to remind myself of the truth, that my Father is not an author of confusion, right? He is good in every way and has only good things for me. He designed me to tune in to His true thoughts that would lead me to a place of feeling loved, knowing I am lovable, and believing that He has someone special who would love every part of me. Out of these truths, I could live every day in my true sexual identity and purity—these truths that would usher me into the destiny my Father planned for me.

What is the lie that swarms around you every day when you look at yourself in the mirror or when you compare yourself to the girls and guys around you? What is that lie that keeps you disconnected from your Father's heart, or causes you to behave out of fear rather than being the young man or young woman that God created you to be? Perhaps you hear this in your head: "I'm not manly looking enough to be desired by a woman" or "I'm not pretty or thin enough

to be desired by a man." Or even the thought I had, "I'm not lovable by the opposite sex?"

With whatever confusing thoughts you're struggling with today, I encourage you to talk to your Heavenly Father. He knows exactly what you're going through and can bring healing into your heart and emotions.

If you are a young woman, He celebrates the goodness of your femininity that you carry. If you are a young man, he celebrates the goodness of your masculinity that you carry! You are Your Father's Treasure.

"We are like common clay jars that carry this glorious treasure within..."
2 Corinthians 4:7 TPT

Challenge

Hear what Father's Heart is toward you:

> "You are engraved on the tablets of my heart.
> You are my masterpiece.
> You are my Treasure.
> My Beloved Son/Daughter
> Victorious and Overcoming One who carries my glory
> You are my Joy and my Delight
> I have a tremendous destiny and purpose for you
> You are my gift to this world and the people in your life.
> You reflect a facet of my glory that only you can reflect.
> I love how I designed you!"

"God had a dream and wrapped your body around it." -Lou Engle

Find a comfortable, quiet space, close your eyes, and ask God to now share with you the truth of how He sees you. Cast aside the stereotypes of what the world says a woman and a man is. Allow God to speak to you His truth of how He sees you! Journal the words of affirmation you receive and God's kind words for you today.

Plan a relaxing time when you can listen to Graham Cooke's video, "Becoming the Beloved". In this video, Graham was inspired to speak encouraging affirmations of what the Father wants you to know about who you are. It has instrumental music in the background.

SEASON OF SINGLENESS

Writing by Charis Logan

"I'm never going to get married! I just don't think that God has someone for me! What is wrong with me?!" I was 24 years old and my older brother had just gotten married and now my younger brother was about to get married. This was NOT how it was supposed to happen.

Upon hearing my lament, my mentor Tisha disclosed an 'equation' that totally shifted my perspective! She shared, "Baby Girl, even if you could get married at 18, but got married at 30, that's 12 years of being single. Say you live until you're 95—that is SIXTY-FIVE years of being a wife! Your season of singleness is drastically shorter than your season of being a wife, so ENJOY it!"

God created us to have relationships. Your Heavenly Father understands your deep longings for connection, and His passion is to bless you. Is it possible to look at your season of singleness as a GIFT from an Amazing Father who sees beyond this moment, sees the bigger picture, and only wants the very best for you? Can you trust that? And even more importantly, can you trust Him? I believe that there are things in your season of singleness that need to be overcome and it's a battle for your purity and intimacy with the Father that really gets set in place, to set you up for an amazing future.

You're not alone. I remember being there and feeling like it was a very bleak season, but I want to encourage you to search out the beauty in the midst of it. There are things in this period of your life that Father God wants to do in you that are meant for right now and will impact all of eternity. He is more than enough for all your needs and always will be. His heart is to lavish His good gifts upon you—so ENJOY it.

Jesus said:

"Steep your life in God-reality, God-initiative, God-provisions. Don't worry about missing out. You'll find all your everyday human concerns will be met."
Matthew 6:33 MSG

Prayer

"Father God, I give You full permission to do all that You want to do in this season of singleness. I give you my feelings of loneliness. I give you my desires. I trust You, Lord, even when it's hard to do. (Hold your hands out in front of you). Father God, what do you have for me during this time of being single?

Challenge

Take time to journal your thoughts, desires, and record anything you sense the Lord speaking to you. You may also sketch a picture of something beautiful and positive that came to your mind in prayer as a word picture of seeing this season in your life.

THE GIFT OF JOYOUS SEX

Writing by Andrew Yasuhara

I couldn't believe it! My best friend was taking the girl of my dreams to senior prom. I had waited for over four years for this moment! And this year I was determined to end my senior year with a bang. (no pun intended)

It all went downhill when Janel, who had coincidentally been in every class that I had senior year, was with me in Florida on our band trip. It was a clear New Year's Eve night and she and I slow danced under the stars. I knew for sure she was the one I would take to senior prom. Everything pointed to this special moment. We had known each other since middle school and now we had almost every class together. We would meet up for study hall and frequently walk from class to class.

It was on one of those walks when I was complaining about how our friends only go to prom to eat dinner and take pictures. They had a bad habit of going to the hotel room and getting wasted. I told Janel, "What's the point of paying all that money for a prom and then not being able to remember the greatest night of senior year?"

It wasn't long until I heard through the grapevine that my best friend had beat me to the punch. He was going with her and I had no one to go with. My one and only shot was down the tubes.

Going to church for most of my life I would always hear about 'true love waits.' I felt like true love had passed me by. My youth pastor would always tell me that sex was a gift from God and I was beginning to believe that gift was for all my friends and not for me. They would come back to school celebrating their one-night stands. And for me, my gift seemed lost in the mail. Was it my fate to die a virgin? Was this the end for me?

Fast forward to the day of my wedding. The moment I laid eyes on Karen as she walked down the aisle, I was overwhelmed. She was the most beautiful

woman I had ever laid my eyes on. She was like a supermodel walking down the runway, and she was coming for me. I'm not kidding, she was gorgeous!

I thought about the heartaches in high school, and I realized that this was my senior prom that I never got to attend. Instead it was thousands of times better!

The gift that I thought I would never have, was good and perfect. And I am so glad I waited for true love.

On my wedding night I experienced the wondrous, joyous, pleasurable, and beautiful gift God had saved for me and my wife to enjoy in a committed marriage relationship. There was such a safety and oneness that only sex in marriage blessed by God brings! It was worth the wait. Sex is also a sacred gift that God makes beautiful in the right time.

"Every good gift and perfect gift is from above, and comes from the Father of lights..." James 1:17 NKJV

Challenge

A special friend of Explicit Movement, Jeremy Byrnes from Nothing Hidden Ministries, shared his thoughts with us on this topic:

"Having amazing sex is about giving. My wife heard from the Lord that having sex is so important, it's spiritually and emotionally bonding and we have to prioritize it. I was, of course, more than okay with this. When I am obeying Holy Spirit's voice, He encourages me to connect with her emotionally and spiritually, which totally turns her on sexually. So, you can see how the reciprocity of giving is a divine recipe for making sex way more than just an orgasm. It's intimacy and ecstasy when Holy Spirit is in the middle of it."

If you still have the gift of your virginity, take a moment to value this precious part of you.

If you have already lost your virginity, know that you can begin anew a life of sexual integrity and purity going forward. As you commit yourself to purity, God sees you as pure. When God's people, Israel, returned to God after giving themselves to other gods, God would view them once again as virgin pure. God is a God of grace as you turn back to Him and His blessed ways.

"I will rebuild you, my virgin Israel. You will again be happy and dance merrily with your tambourines." Jeremiah 31:4 NLT

Take a few moments now to reflect on this elevated view of sex within God's design and meditate on God's hopes, dreams, and intention for you regarding His gift of sex. Surrender your own view of sex up to this point and ask the Lord to impart to you His perspectives and values—a compass for your decisions and choices going forward. God is for you, and He wants to bless you with His best. You are worth the wait, and your purity is worth protecting.

Consider journaling a prayer of your hopes and desires regarding this topic.

Faithful. True. Steadfast. Becoming fully
devoted to God is a response to His devotion
to you. As we end this 21-day journey,
a few last stepping stones have been placed
before you so you may continue to become like
a surefooted deer, rising higher and standing
secure on mountain heights as He declares,

"Behold the radiant beauty of
My Devoted One!"

———

/devoted_

Those who have lived in darkness, are often those that cling to the light with the deepest devotion.

Step into my story, these secret pages of my past. If Jesus can free and heal me from the chains of torment, He can do the same for you.

I vaguely remember those days past. Suffocating darkness gripping the deepest parts of me. Controlled by voices of evil whispering, "There is no hope, no way out, no relief." Exhausted and locked in a prison of despair. My soul cried out, "Help!" But speechless as my voice was silenced by the controlling voices that shouted louder than I. I was alone, unloved, and forgotten.

One day, as I walked down a dusty road in the marketplace, I found myself suddenly caught in a crowd of people pressing toward something or someone as if it was of great importance. Inner voices in me screamed, "Get away!" But deep down, a place that had been silenced for years began to cry out "Move closer." I forcefully took steps through the crowd while being tormented by my inner demons.

Then, He appeared like a piercing light into my soul. Love, compassion, authority, and power. A Presence I had never felt before. His name was JESUS! With every ounce of strength, I shouted, "Jesus!" Jesus then approached me and commanded the demons to leave me! Instantly, the darkness fled, the chains lifted, and the prison doors opened. Freedom!

Everything changed for me in that moment. I owed this man my life. I made a vow to follow Him no matter what.

As the months passed, I never imagined the things I would see as I followed Jesus. Blind eyes opened, leprosy healed, the dead raised. He was more than just a miracle worker, He was my Lord.

I was there when they brutally nailed Him to the cross. Two days later, I hesitantly made my way to the tomb to honor His memory. In utter shock, the tomb was empty! Who took his body? Then I heard a familiar voice. Could it be? Jesus was alive!

Oh, how He longs for an ever-deepening friendship with you. Such is the experience of those faithful, loyal, and devoted to Him, the One worthy of it all!

✖

A creative narrative written by Shannon Marocco, based on Mary Magdalene found in Luke 8:1-3, John 19:25, John 20:11-18

OPEN

Writing by Damon Gohata

Vulnerable. Weak. Powerless. Who would want these words to describe them? I certainly didn't, but how are you supposed to feel when you are pulling yourself out of a trash can after being mistaken for a 7th grader by a classmate when I was 13? I hated the way I felt about myself, so I used accomplishments to build walls around my heart to protect it from the pain.

I got pretty good at building walls too. By age 35, I had the life I had always dreamed about growing up. I had all of my boxes checked. Still going to church every week. Check. Graduated College. Check. Completed seminary school. Check. On church staff. Check. Running a relatively successful business. Check. Hot wife, 3 kids, house. Check, check, check. I was living the life I wanted, so why was it that most of the year I was having panic attacks, anxious about my marriage, my business, my relationships, and feeling totally disconnected from other people and God?

I realized that the walls I built did not heal my heart, they just hid it. Walls don't discriminate, they keep everything out. I had built so many walls in my life to protect my heart from pain, but they also kept me from being able to fully be loved by God or by anyone else. Somewhere I believed that my accomplishments and checking off all my boxes would bring fulfillment and bring me closer to God.

God wants my heart, not my walls. There is power in vulnerability. Being real with yourself, others you trust, and God. Vulnerability is a vital ingredient in developing intimacy with God in your journey through life.

The Lord LOVES to break through our walls. Beloved, behind those walls lies the seeds of the treasure within you that God wants to release through you. Yes, it is scary! Yes, it feels safer and more comfortable behind the walls we build, but with courage and God's power, healing and transformation awaits you—and an intimacy with the Lord that are like deep waters.

Did you know you can be angry with God and express it to him? His heart is so huge, and He already understands you so completely, that you are NEVER too much for Him. You can lament and weep to Him, laugh and dance with Him, and share with Him your deepest secrets and fears. He wants you to simply come as you are to Him. No performance necessary or wanted. He just wants you.

Open the door of your heart to Him—He is your safe place. God loves you so much that you can come to Him just as you are. His relentless love for you will mature and grow you into who you were created to be. Come and just 'be' in His Presence. He awaits you!

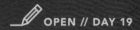
"Behold, I'm standing at the door, knocking. If your heart is open to hear my voice and you open the door within, I will come in to you and feast with you, and you will feast with me." Revelation 3:20 TPT

Prayer

"Dear Lord, reveal to me the things in my life that are getting in between you and I. I have tried to protect my heart from pain, and in the process have built walls that have kept your love out. I want to live as your Beloved Son/Daughter. Help me trust that you are good, and that I can lay my walls down before you so that I can receive all that you have for me. Jesus, I open the door of my heart to you and invite you in. Amen."

Challenge

Fear of emotional pain is a major reason that we build walls to hide behind. Our hearts are tender, and we want to protect them. Social media can be a great communication tool, but it can also be a good way to hide and only show off the "best" side of ourselves. Today, take a break from social media and spend the time that you would normally spend on social media and go somewhere quiet (a park, the beach, etc.) and be with God.

A further step you can take is to initiate spending time with someone you feel safe with, who is a good listener, and who would encourage you in your walk with the Lord. If you do not have such a person currently in your life, ask the Lord to highlight someone that could be that godly confidant and initiate spending time with that person and sharing some of your burdens.

Consider journaling a prayer to God expressing your innermost emotions and thoughts about where your heart is right now—practice being open and vulnerable with God.

TRUST

Writing by John Allison

"Am I enough?"

It was a simple question, but I knew what God was asking. I have wanted to be married and have a family since I was four years old. God was asking me if He was enough for me even if I never got married. He was asking if He was more important to me than my childhood dreams. God was asking me to trust Him by letting go of my plans and putting my life in His hands.

In order to follow him, I needed to lay down my plans and pick up God's plans for me. God knows me. He knows my desires to have a family. Those are good, holy desires! Yet, He wanted to be first in my life, even above my dreams.

Many things in my life have competed with God for the first place. Some are good desires, like having a family, and some selfish. God was reminding me that no matter how good my plans are, His are better.

When I shared my struggle with my friend, he pointed me to two places in the Bible where God makes powerful promises to those who remain single for God's kingdom. He asked if I was willing to trust that God had a better plan for me—even if it wasn't what I would choose for myself?

Jesus says the only way to find true life is to give our life to him. The more tightly I cling to my plans, the more likely I am to make a mess of my life. However, when I surrender those desires to Jesus and trust Him to lead me, I start truly living.

I had to learn that trust is a daily habit. Do you think I had to give Him my childhood dreams only once? Of course not! Trusting Jesus doesn't just happen once, but every day.

The most important piece of the puzzle came when I discovered Psalm 16:11. It promises that my deepest happiness and greatest pleasure is found in the presence of Jesus. When I trust Him, I exchange small, temporary pleasures

for huge, eternal ones. Following Jesus, will lead me to what I truly need: Him. It's in that relationship that I am truly set free.

It gets even better! Over the years He has given me spiritual children through mentorship, spiritual mothers who welcomed me into their homes, and spiritual grandparents who gave generously to me. God's better plan for you may include a spouse and a family, or it may be very different than what you imagine.

Maybe you have a financial issue, relationship, school application, or job interview that you have hopes for. The point is not to throw those hopes away, but to entrust them to a God who knows you, loves you, and has your best interest at heart.

Can you trust Him? Is He enough? I've had to answer that question many times, and each time I become more confident that He is. I don't know what the future holds, and He may still have a wife and family for me, but I do know that I must trust Him for today. Jesus is truly enough.

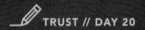
"Trust in the LORD with all your heart, and do not lean on your own understanding. In all your ways acknowledge him, and he will make straight your paths."
Proverbs 3:5-6 ESV

"Restlessness and impatience change nothing except our peace and joy. Peace does not dwell in outward things, but in the heart prepared to wait trustfully and quietly on him who has all things safely in his hands." - Elizabeth Elliot

Challenge

Imagine a long, straight road through the countryside. On either side of the road are two wooden fences. Following Jesus is like running down that road. Sometimes we get distracted by what's on the other side of the fence and forget that we have the freedom to run forever along the road.

Spend some time asking the Holy Spirit to show you the things in your life that are "on the other side of the fence." Write them here and ask Him to help you entrust those things to Jesus. Also ask Him to fill you with joy as you run down the road toward freedom and deeper intimacy with Jesus.

When possible, listen to the song, "I Surrender" sung by Kim Walker (Jesus Culture), worship Him, and give your all to Jesus!

DEVOTED

Writing by Tisha Lehfeldt

It's day 21 and you are about to complete this journal! Congratulations on being incredibly devoted. And yes, that is the word we want to leave you with. Devoted. Being devoted is a critical part of our faith and journey with God. Devotion happens when we are convinced at the core of our being that God loves us, is for us, and we love Him back with all our heart. And knowing His heart, following Him, and becoming like Him will be our number one pursuit.

My life of devotion towards God started 31 years ago—a decision that completely transformed me. I threw a stake in the ground that day and said, "I'm gonna be a person who follows and honors God with all my heart!"

As we say our goodbyes, I want to introduce you to a man who inspires me. His name is Shammah, known as one of King David's mighty men:

"...When the Philistines banded together at a place where there was a field full of lentils, Israel's troops fled from them. But Shammah took his stand in the middle of the field. He defended it and struck the Philistines down, and the Lord brought about a great victory." 2 Samuel 23:11-12 NIV

This field full of lentils belonged to the Israelites. It was a source of their food and livelihood. Notice that all Shammah's fellow Israelites fled in fear. However, Shammah took his stand in the middle of the field, defended it, and struck down the enemy.

The question is, will you be like the Israelites running in fear and intimidation? Or will you be like Shammah, getting in the middle of your field, fighting the enemy at hand and defending it? What is your field full of lentils? Your field beloved, is your relationship with God, your calling, your relationships, your heavenly identity, your sexual purity, and more. Shammah didn't stand on the side, in the back or on the fringe of the field—he stood smack dab in the middle of the field and fought against those who wanted to steal and destroy!

God is looking for Shammahs in this generation. Audacious men and women full of grit, resolution and boldness. Someone devoted to God by honoring Him with their heart, mind, bodies, choices and decisions. Beloved, will you take a stand and fight for a close relationship with God, others, and your calling? Your field is worth the battle. In Him, you will be victorious and glorious.

When you find yourself in the heat of the battles, take your stand. Don't run. Stand because you know what you stand for and the WHY behind it! You are not alone. You are a part of a powerful generation that is devoted to God. A collection of people that will be none like this planet has ever seen before!

May the Lord impart to you a supernatural courage, massive favor, grace, hope, patience, forgiveness, healing, restoration, wisdom, joy, vision and unflinching love! May you be a son/daughter grounded in the Father's love for the display of His splendor!

May the Lord impart to you a supernatural courage, massive favor, grace, hope, patience, forgiveness, healing, restoration, wisdom, joy, vision and unflinching love! May you be a son/daughter grounded in the Father's love for the display of His splendor!

Challenge

Review this journal from time to time to remind yourself who God says you are and what God says you can do. I declare over you:

"Be on your guard; stand firm in the faith; be courageous; be strong. Do everything in love." 1 Corinthians 16:13-14 NIV

Go into a quiet room and position yourself near one of the walls. Ask the Holy Spirit to reveal what is the field you are fighting for, such as your relationship with God, a relationship with someone close to you, your sexual purity, your God given identity, or your calling.

Close your eyes and envision yourself at the fringe of a real field. It's your field. The field you're fighting for. Now slowly take a few steps into the middle of the room. As you do, picture yourself walking into the middle of your field. Once in the middle, take a deep breath and say this out loud:

"This is my field. I'm throwing the stake down. This field will not be taken by the enemy—not on my watch! I will stand here and fight the enemy, I will not run! My _____ (life, relationship with God, singleness, sexual integrity, ministry/calling etc.) matters to you and me, God. Lord, give me the strength, wisdom and power to fight. Together we will stand in the middle, fight this battle, and win!"

Lift your hands in surrender and praise to God. Begin to ask God to fill you with new strength, new grit, new courage and new resolution to be the person He has intended for you to be! Devote yourself to fully live life His way!

Journal your final reflections.

Plan a time when you can meditate and listen to the worship medley, "Oceans/You Make Me Brave" by Caleb and Kelsey. Allow the Lord to impart to you His courage and strength for the journey!

SMALL GROUP
DISCUSSION QUESTIONS

This section of discussion questions is a resource for leaders/facilitators of youth groups, young adult groups, and other small groups to help readers process through each devotional more deeply. Our hope is that as groups discuss, participants will gain more insights, connect heart to heart with each other, learn from and support one another, and experience God at work in their lives.

The journal is broken into five different sections. Depending on the amount of time available, either one devotional, part of a section, or an entire section can be discussed in one sitting.

The following can be used as helpful ice-breaker starters to begin each discussion:

What stood out to you from this devotional? (or which devotional stood out to you the most in this section and why?)

- **What do you sense God is saying to you?**
- **What is a take-away?**
- **If you did the 'challenge activity' following the devotional, feel free to share your experience.**

DAY 1: THIRST

1. "What I don't understand about myself is that I decide one way, but then I act another, doing things I absolutely despise." Romans 7:15 MSG

   One of the greatest mysteries in life is why we continually find sin more attractive and entertaining than the Presence of God. Even Apostle Paul, a hero of the faith, struggled. What are some desires that take your time and focus from God?

2. One of the greatest challenges is trying to change our desires. Often times change only happens when the pain of not changing exceeds the fear of change.

   What have been some negative outcomes of a decision you have made apart from God? What did you learn from that experience?

3. What have been some positive outcomes of a decision you made as you sought God's wisdom and ways? What did these positive outcomes teach you?

4. Jesus promises that when we drink of the water He gives us, we will never thirst again. What do you think it looks like to drink of the water Jesus offers and never thirst again? Describe a time you were completely satisfied in Jesus.

DAY 2: IN SEARCH

1. When we come into this world it doesn't catch God off guard. He isn't thinking, "What am I going to do with you?" Instead, the Bible says He has beautiful plans for our life before we're even conceived. Why do you think the devil wants to keep you from fulfilling God's plans for your life?

   "Before I shaped you in the womb, I knew all about you. Before you saw the light of day, I had holy plans for you: A prophet to the nations— that's what I had in mind for you." Jeremiah 1:5 MSG

2. The Bible says we are God's handiwork. The word 'handiwork' is a translation from the Greek word poiēma. Sound familiar? It's where we get the word 'poem'. In other words, you are like a beautiful and unique work of poetry that God intimately crafted. What words, thoughts, or feelings come to mind when you meditate on the idea of God scripting your being like poetry?

"For we are God's handiwork, created in Christ Jesus to do good works, which God prepared in advance for us to do." Ephesians 2:10 NIV

3. God's Word makes it clear that He created you with a specific plan in mind. The closer we walk to God's plan for our life the more rewarding and fulfilling life becomes. What do you believe God would have you do in this moment to discover more of His plan for you?

4. If you have an inkling to what your future calling may be, please share. If you do not have a sense of direction for your calling yet, share about a dream you have. Sometimes the dreams in our heart may give us clues to our calling.

DAY 3: FINALLY FULFILLED

1. Have you ever craved something you knew wasn't good for you? If so, share what that was and why it wasn't good for you.

What is one thing currently in your life that you desire to stop craving after or doing (or at least decrease the amount of time you devote to it) because you know it is not healthy or good for you? Why is this highlighted to you?

2. "Blessed are those who hunger and thirst for righteousness, for they will be filled." Matthew 5:6 NIV

Jesus promises that when we crave the right things, our desires will be satisfied. What does it look like for you to hunger and thirst for righteousness (God's right ways)? What are some actions that can keep you connected to God's heart and following His ways?

3. Do you have a story from your life that illustrates how you experienced God's blessings when you desired to follow His ways and did? If so, please share.

4. The phrase in Matthew 5:6, "will be filled" literally means, "to fulfill or satisfy the desire of". Why do you think desiring God and His righteousness fulfills and satisfies us?

5. So many things in life offer temporary fulfillment and satisfaction but Jesus is the only one who offers Himself as a limitless source of perfect fulfillment and wholeness. What step would God have you take today to enter deeper into that promise?

SECTION 2: BREAKING SHAME

DAY 4: RESTORED

1. What are your thoughts and feelings about sexual trauma/abuse?

2. Do you know anyone personally who has experienced sexual abuse, physical abuse or verbal abuse? If so, how did their experience impact you?

3. In what ways can God make 'everything beautiful in His time' regarding trauma?

4. What was your experience during the challenge activity?

DAY 5: THE GREAT EXCHANGE

1. What is a lie you've believed about yourself that has prevented you from fully living according to God's will?

2. Can you think of a moment when this lie first became real to you? If you can recall a moment and you feel comfortable sharing, describe this moment with the group.

3. What is one truth that God wants you to know and believe?

4. The group can end the time by praying for one another to receive and believe the one truth (shared in question 3) that God wants each person to embrace.

DAY 6: HOPE AND HEALING

1. Every person has areas in their life that God wants to heal and transform. What would be some hindrances in sharing vulnerably with a church leader or a brother or sister in Christ about any hidden struggles with temptations and sins you have?

2. When we hide our struggles from others and avoid seeking help to overcome them, our relationships with the Lord and others are affected. We can become isolated and alone. God's healing light is not able to touch what we purposely hide in darkness. In what ways does hiding our struggles affect us emotionally? Spiritually? Physically

3. If you had an experience when your vulnerability was met with awkwardness, hurtful silence, or judgement, please share what that was like for you. How did that affect the feeling of shame you had prior to sharing?

4. If you have a positive testimony of a time when your vulnerability was met with grace and love, please share what that was like for you. How did that help? How did this affect the feeling of shame you had prior to sharing?

5. What are some ways can God minister hope to those who are in pain, shame, and despair? What is God's heart towards those walking in shame?

DAY 7: FREEDOM

1. How have you wanted the world to view you?

2. What, if any, is a fear you currently struggle with? Because of that fear, how do you try to control things?

3. What is a positive TRUTH that God has told you in the past about who you are? If you have a hard time believing that truth, why do you struggle with receiving this truth?

4. Take turns in your small group and share with each person how everyone else sees him/her—how God sees them. This is a time of positively affirming one another's value and expressing appreciation for who each person is.

DAY 8: FINDING HOME

1. What are the qualities of a person that you would feel safe being vulnerable with?

   If you have a safe person in your life, what makes them safe? What are qualities you appreciate about him/her?

2. What are the qualities that a small group would need to have in order for you to feel comfortable enough to be vulnerable and open in your sharing?

3. Knowing being vulnerable is taking a risk, what would be some concerns you would have in being vulnerable with a person or group?

4. Keeping in mind that no person, family, or group is perfect, describe the type of community you would want to belong to.

SECTION 3: VICTORIOUS LOVE

DAY 9: CHOOSING LOVE

1. When faced with choosing between love or lust in a challenging moment, what would be some helpful perspectives to keep in mind that would motivate you to choose love?

2. What does it look like for you to live every day out of a deep place of love for others so that when temptation comes along, you would not waiver?

3. What would be some helpful key questions you could ask yourself to help you guard your own sexual integrity?

4. If you have a testimony where you experienced a breakthrough/victory over a type of lust you struggled with, please share.

5. Is there an area of lust that you currently struggle with? (it could be sexual lust, lust after power, lust after material things, etc.)?
   If so, (if you feel comfortable) share your burden and ask for prayer.

6. You may end the group time by praying for one another regarding any needs expressed.

DAY 10: INTO THE LIGHT

1. In your house or room, where do you hide your clutter? How often do you clean it out? Does this in any way relate to how you deal with issues in your life you know need to be worked on? If so, how?

2. Share about a memorable experience you had when someone supported you through a difficult time or helped you work through a challenging issue. How did this person help you? How did you see God at work?

3. What are some areas of your life that you could use support in?

4. Do you have a person or a few people in your life who support you and keep you accountable in your walk with Christ? If yes, share what you appreciate about their support.

5. If you currently do not have a spiritual mentor who is supporting you and helping you keep accountable, who might be a person or a few people you could approach to fill that spiritual father or mother role in your life?

DAY 11: PURE

1. How do you feel about the issue of pornography? What are some of your thoughts about this issue?

2. If you have viewed porn before, when was the first time you viewed porn? How did you feel? What did you do afterwards?

3. If you struggle with porn, what are things you are doing to resist temptation and to stay accountable?

4. In what ways can our community become a safer place for others to confess their secret battle with porn or any addiction?

DAY 12: PLEASURE YOURSELF

1. What are some things you do for your pleasure? Is what you're doing to pleasure yourself beneficial to your walk with God? Explain why or why not.

2. Is the source of your pleasure in God or in sin? Explain why this is so.

3. Is what you are doing for pleasure bringing you positive benefits or harm? Share the ways it benefits you or harms you.

DAY 13: LET LOVE BE YOUR HIGHEST GOAL

1. When was a time that you felt really loved (not necessarily with a significant other)? What made it so special?

2. Love is more than a feeling; it's a choice. In order for a person to feel loved, we must love them the way they feel loved, and that's why it's hard! If you are familiar with Gary Chapman's Five Love Languages (Words of Affirmation, Acts of Service, Quality Time, Gifts, Physical Touch & Closeness), what are your top two "love languages"?

3. Brainstorm ways to say "I love you," or even "I like you," without getting physical or sexually involved with someone.

SECTION 4: FATHER'S HEART

DAY 14: FATHER'S AFFIRMATION

1. What are some attributes of a good, earthly father?

2. What are some positive traits of your father (or someone who is a father figure in your life as a grandfather, uncle, mentor, or teacher) that you appreciate?

3. If you can, recall a special, memorable, positive memory with your father or a father figure. Share what came to mind and why it blessed you.

4. In looking at your own life, do you see the influence of your father? In what ways has this been displayed?

5. Take a look at the following list of some descriptions of Father God. Pick one of your favorites and share why you appreciate the particular characteristic you chose.

Abundantly Available	Loving/Compassionate
Answering God	Encourager
Advocate	Faithful/Trustworthy
Gracious/Forgiving	Hiding Place/Refuge
Almighty/Powerful	Provider
Guide/Wise Counselor	Listener
Protector	Refreshing/Reviving
Generous Giver	Glorious/Beautiful

DAY 15: GOOD FATHER

1. The Bible tells us that God is even better than any earthly father.

   Read this passage:

   "Do you know of any parent who would give his hungry child, who asked for food, a plate of rocks instead? Or when asked for a piece of fish, what parent would offer his child a snake instead? If you, imperfect as you are, know how to lovingly take care of your children and give them what's best, how much more ready is your heavenly Father to give wonderful gifts to those who ask him?" Matthew 7:9-11 TPT

   How does this passage change what you think about God's intentions and heart toward you? What is highlighted to you?

2. What is a way (or some ways) you have experienced God through a father figure in your life?

3. Reflect on the past year—was there any blessing you received that was memorable and could be attributed to God's favor and love for you? If so, share that experience.

DAY 16: TREASURE

1. Share 3 positive qualities and 3 weaknesses you are aware of about yourself.

2. Share what the stereotypical worldly views are about femininity and masculinity.

3. Contrast the worldly view of femininity and masculinity with God's view. In general, what are feminine qualities of a godly woman and the masculine qualities of a godly man? (many qualities may overlap)

DAY 17: SEASON OF SINGLENESS

1. What do you feel is the hardest part about being single?

2. How have you seen God provide for your needs (emotional, physical, spiritual, etc.) during this season of singleness?

3. Rather than only asking God why you're single, take a moment to ask Him what He has for you in this season of singleness. Share some things that come to mind with your group.

DAY 18: THE JOYOUS GIFT OF SEX

1. Before reading this journal, what was your view of sex? What is your view now?

2. How do you feel about waiting until marriage to have sex?

3. Knowing that God created sex for pleasure within marriage, how does this affect your view on sex?

4. How important do you think sex within marriage is? Explain your answer.

5. What questions about sex do you have after reading this devotional?

DAY 19: OPEN

1. Which of these statements do you connect in your heart with more? Share why you chose that statement.

    a. God is going to judge me.
    b. God loves me unconditionally and desires for me experience more of His joy and freedom.

2. Think of a past experience that caused you to build and hide behind walls with people and/or God. If you feel comfortable enough, briefly describe that situation with your group.

3. In what ways does being open and vulnerable with God affect your intimacy with Him? How would being vulnerable with God affect your devotion to Him?

4. Tell the group one thing that you are afraid of. After everyone in the group has shared, discuss if sharing fears led to a feeling of connection or disconnection with the other members of the group. How did you feel when each person shared with some level of vulnerability with the group?

5. Share about a time when your experienced God's deep love for you.

DAY 20: TRUST

1. How important is trust in a close relationship?
   Why does Jesus want us to trust and follow Him?

2. What is one thing you have a difficult time trusting the Lord with? Why do you think that is the case?

3. Is there an area of your life where you find it easy to trust the Lord? What are some of those things?

4. Do you have a testimony of when you trusted God and He came through in faithfulness? Please share.

5. What are some specific ways you can help each other trust Jesus with the things you have shared?

DAY 21: DEVOTED

1. The Philistines were the Israelites' enemy and wanted to steal their life from them. In what ways do you see the enemy trying to steal your life, your relationship with God and others, your purity, or your calling?

2. Share a time you were like Shammah and had the guts to take a stand?

3. Share about a time when you wanted to quit, give up, or run and not do life God's way (i.e., unforgiveness, indifference, impurity, etc.)?

4. What steps can you take to resist the attacks of the enemy to stay devoted to God and His ways?

ACKNOWLEDGEMENTS

The Explicit Movement 21-Day Interactive Journal could not have turned from a dream into reality without all those who generously contributed their time and talents to make it possible. Thank you to all the brilliant authors who shared their wisdom and God stories that inspire great hope and healing. Thank you to Jensen Hirayama for help with editing, Austin Lord of Austin Lord Photography for contributing the photo for Day 7, Seth Buckley for contributing the photo for Day 10, and Catalyst Christian Community for their generous support towards this project. Thank you to Sakura Reese and Ahava Design for putting all the pieces together with a visual impact that truly is a work of art. Above all, we thank the Lord for His vision and inspiration to see people around the world transformed with faith, hope and love.

ABOUT EXPLICIT MOVEMENT

Youth and young adults around the world are hurting with insecurity about their identity and are often confused when it comes to sex and relationships. Their struggle is intensified by distorted views of sexuality promoted by the media, school curriculums, pornography, and the entertainment industry.

THE CAUSE

Explicit Movement seeks to influence the surrounding culture to embrace and celebrate God's design for sex as a beautiful and amazing gift reserved for marriage between one man and one woman.

Our vision is to see youth and young adults around the world living with sexual integrity and leading others to do the same.

OUR APPROACH

We seek to:

- Help establish people's identity in Christ and their relationship with God.
- Heal hearts from hurts and shame with God's power, love, and truth.
- Equip people with tools to protect their sexual integrity and to live out healthy relationships.

THE GOAL OF TRANSFORMATION

Saving sex for marriage helps to build a firm foundation for strong marriages, which in turn builds healthy families, communities and nations. Embracing godly, healthy, sexuality is just one facet in bringing God's transformation to a person, city or nation, but it is an important one.

Mikela Kobayashi, a youth pastor on our speaker team, said it best:

"Marriages are the foundation to families, and families are the foundation to communities, cities, and nations. Dating lives are the foundation to marriages, so essentially dating lives can transform a nation."

WHAT MAKES EXPLICIT MOVEMENT UNIQUE?

GRACE-FILLED ENVIRONMENT: We create a safe, disarming environment at conference events through the speakers' vulnerability and tenor of their messages that communicate grace and truth. Attendees experience healing from pain and shame, encouragement and hope for new beginnings.

BODY OF CHRIST EFFORT: Explicit Movement Conferences are catalytic events that bring churches and the host community together. Churches partner in unity together to impact their region. Core teams of pastors and leaders from various churches and denominations contribute their gifts and expertise to the events and to their local Explicit Movement branch.

PARENT INVOLVEMENT: Parents are often at a loss for answers on how to influence their child's heart. We equip parents to build a positive connection with their children and how to meaningfully engage with them on topics of healthy sexuality.

EQUIPPING LEADERS: We provide pre-event and post-event workshops for pastors and leaders. Pastors and leaders are able to build relationships, support one another and be resources to each other. We are also developing resources and curriculum for churches.

GLOBAL NETWORK: We are developing partnerships with Christian leaders in their respective regions and nations. We believe our calling is to serve the Body of Christ globally wherever God would send us.

HOW CAN WE SERVE YOU?

We would love to meet with you to hear what God is doing in your region and collaborate to tailor an Explicit Movement event with follow-up strategies that meet your needs.

We are also developing a library of resources for youth, young adults, church leaders and parents.

JOIN THE MOVEMENT!

WOULD YOU PARTNER WITH US?

The Lord has the world on His mind and heart! Would you prayerfully consider partnering with Explicit Movement as we seek to impact the youth, young adults and families of the world? Let's lift up the cause together and leave a legacy for generations to come!

CONTACT US

info@explicitmovement.org

LEARN MORE AT

www.explicitmovement.org

FACEBOOK

Explicit Movement Hawaii

YOUTUBE

Explicit Movement

INSTAGRAM

explicitmovementhawaii